AlphaBasiCs

Sports
from A to Z

Bobbie Kalman & Kate Calder

Crabtree Publishing Company

AlphaBasiCs

Created by Bobbie Kalman

To Bob Perry, an aspiring athlete

Editor-in-Chief
Bobbie Kalman

Writing team
Bobbie Kalman
Kate Calder

Managing editor
Lynda Hale

Editors
Jane Lewis
Heather Levigne

Computer design
Lynda Hale

Production coordinator
Hannelore Sotzek

Separations and film
Dot 'n Line Image Inc.

Printer
Worzalla Publishing Company

Special thanks to
Paul Lewis, Ridley College Archives; Judy Joubert, Sport By Ability Niagara; Linda Weigl & Warren Rylands; David Cosgrove, Andrew Corolis, and the Ridley College Middle School hockey team; Ridley College; Samantha Crabtree; Jay Hedden; Earl Haig Public School; Futures Gymnastics Center

Photographs
Marc Crabtree: pages 8 (top), 10 (right), 12, 17 (left), 22 (top right); Judy Joubert: page 20 (top); Bobbie Kalman: pages 6 (all except top right), 26 (right); Bob Langrish: page 11; Diane Payton Majumdar: page 23 (top & right); courtesy of Ridley College Archives: page 24 (top left); SportsChrome: page 18 (top right); Giuliano Bevilacqua/SportsChrome: page 31; Brian Drake/SportsChrome: page 16 (top); Rüdiger Fessel/SportsChrome: page 19 (bottom); Caroline Indberdorf & Claudia Peczinka/SportsChrome: page 26 (left); Frank Peters/SportsChrome: page 19 (top left); Bob Tringali/SportsChrome: page 18 (bottom right); Robert Tringali/SportsChrome: pages 7, 20 (bottom), 22 (bottom right); Chip Isenhart/Tom Stack & Associates: page 15; Eric Sanford/Tom Stack & Associates: page 28; Linda Weigl: pages 17 (bottom right), 24 (top right); other images by Digital Stock and Eyewire, Inc.

Crabtree Publishing Company

PMB 16A
350 Fifth Avenue,
Suite 3308
New York, NY
10118

360 York Road,
RR 4
Niagara-on-the-Lake,
Ontario, Canada
L0S 1J0

73 Lime Walk
Headington
Oxford
OX3 7AD
United Kingdom

Cataloging in Publication Data
Kalman, Bobbie
  Sports from A to Z

(AlphaBasiCs)
Includes index.

ISBN 0-86505-386-3 (library bound) ISBN 0-86505-416-9 (pbk.)
This book is an alphabetical introduction to various aspects of sports, using such words as "Active," "Exercise," "Lacrosse," "Olympics," and "Soccer."

1. Sports—Juvenile literature. 2. English language—Alphabet—Juvenile literature. [1. Sports. 2. Alphabet.] I. Calder, Kate. II. Title. III. Series: Kalman, Bobbie. AlphaBasiCs.

GV705.4.K35 1999   j796   LC 99-23767
                                                        CIP

Contents

A is for **active**. Being active means moving your body instead of sitting around. Running, skipping, and playing are all ways that you can be active. **Athletes** are active. They play sports and keep their body strong by exercising. Do you play sports? Do you skip, stretch, run, and jump? Being active is fun and healthy. How many ways have you been active today?

B is for **basketball**. Basketball is a team sport played on a marked area called a **court**, shown below. Five players on each team take turns **dribbling**, or bouncing, and passing the ball while they move down the court. They run, dodge, and turn to get past their **opponents**. The object of the game is to make points by shooting the ball through a basket that hangs at the other team's end of the court. Shooting the ball through the basket takes practice. How many baskets can you make?

C is for **circus arts**. Circus arts such as clown antics and **trapeze** moves are fun to do and watch. The Spanish web is a rope act in which an acrobat, or performer, moves with skill on a hanging rope. He or she hangs by her wrist or ankle from a loop on the rope while performing. A person called a web-setter stands below to control and spin the rope. Circus performers practice their routines carefully and safely. They must have excellent balance and strength.

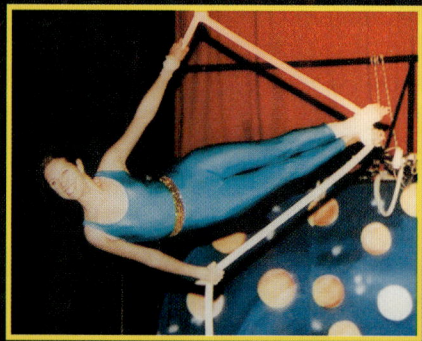

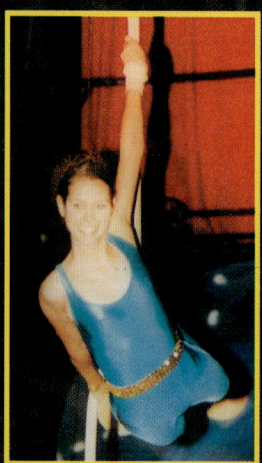

is for **diving**. Divers jump into the water from platforms as high as 30 feet (9 m)—which is higher than a two-story house! They twist, turn, somersault, and tuck their body in the air. When they enter the water, divers must keep their body as straight as possible so they do not make a splash. In a competition, judges mark the divers on the difficulty of their dive and how well they do it. The more difficult the dive, the more points the diver can earn.

E is for **exercise**. Everyone needs to exercise. Exercising helps us stay healthy and strong. Athletes exercise to get better at their sport. They lift weights to build their muscles. Many people run or swim to help make their heart stronger. You can exercise by playing tag, skipping rope, or riding your bike. Exercising will help you run longer, jump higher, and pedal faster!

(above) Stretching before you exercise warms up your muscles. Warming up your muscles helps prevent injuries.

(bottom left and right) Jumping into a pool or playing a game of field hockey are both fun ways to exercise.

F is for **football**. Football is a popular sport in North America. Every week millions of football fans go to large **stadiums** to watch their favorite teams compete. Each team tries to pass and carry the ball across the other team's goal line and score a touchdown. Football is a **contact sport**. Players tackle their opponents to prevent them from making a touchdown. Football players wear protective padding under their uniform to keep from getting hurt. For fun you can play touch football or flag football. Instead of tackling, players touch their opponents or grab a piece of fabric from their uniform to prevent them from making a touchdown.

*Football players wear **cleats**. Cleats are shoes with spikes on the bottom that grip the ground when the players run. In which other sports do the players wear cleats?*

G is for **gymnastics**. Gymnastics are exercises that require a lot of strength, balance, and flexibility. Many **routines**, or series of moves, are performed on mats or a cushioned floor. Some are performed on an **apparatus** such as rings, uneven bars, the balance beam, or a trampoline. Can you do a somersault, handstand, or the splits? These are basic gymnastic moves.

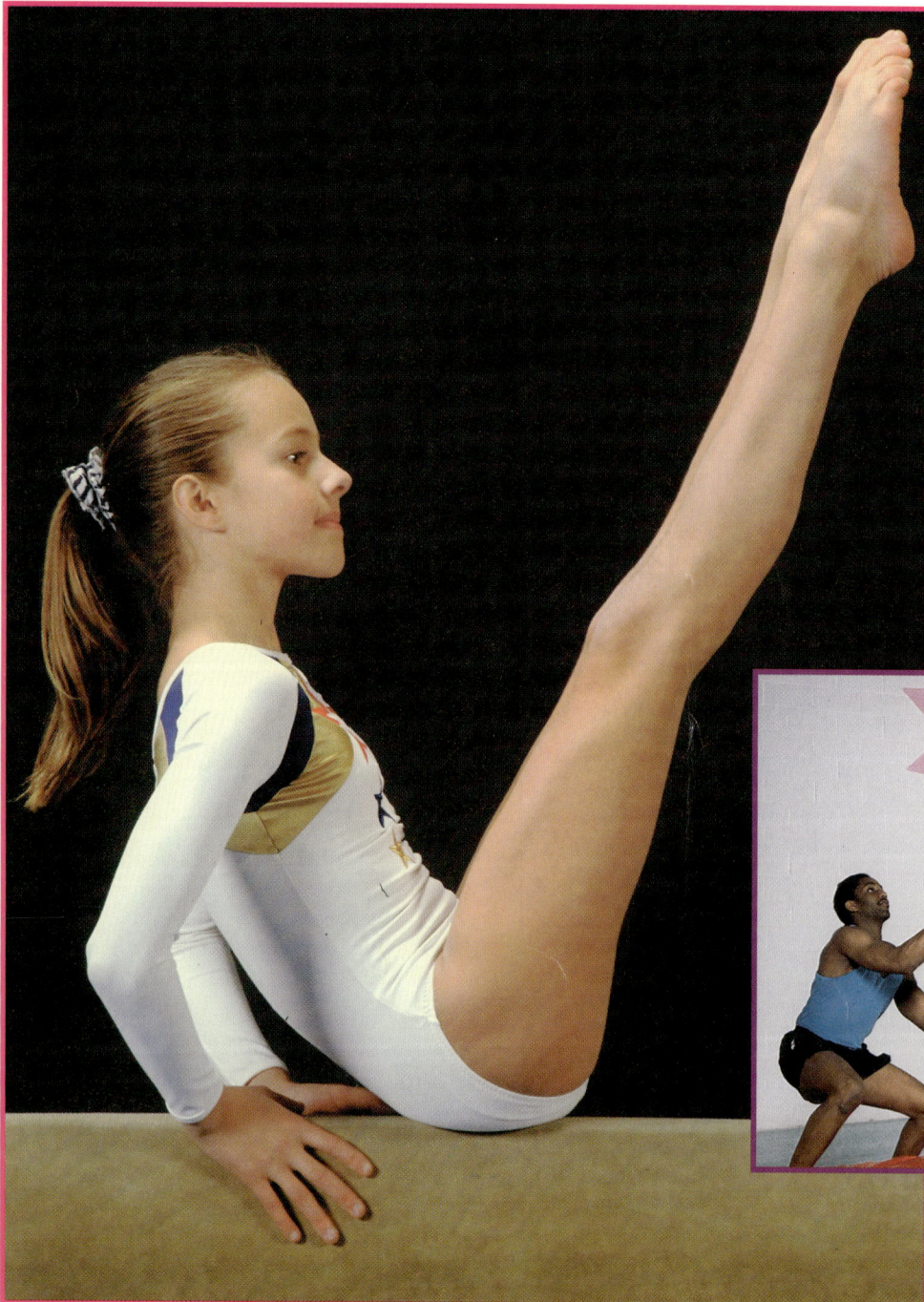

*Gymnasts perform daring flips and turns on an apparatus. The girl to the left is holding a position on the balance beam. The boy below is practicing a jump from a trampoline. His coach is **spotting** him, or making sure the gymnast will not fall or injure himself.*

H is for **horseback riding**. **Equestrians** ride horses in events such as show jumping, dressage, and steeplechase. In show jumping, riders guide their horse around an obstacle course. The horse jumps over grass hedges, wooden bars, stone walls, and water holes. The horse and rider who make it through the course the fastest, and without knocking over any bars or falling, win first prize.

*This horse has a bridle and reins that the rider pulls to steer or stop the horse. The rider wears a riding jacket and tight-fitting pants called **breeches**. Riders must wear a hard riding hat to protect their head in case of a fall.*

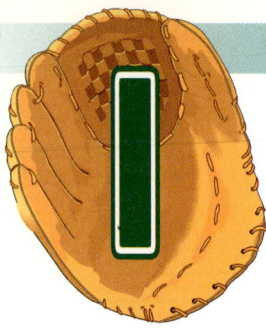

I is for **ice**. **Hockey** is played on an ice rink. It is a fast-moving sport. Players on skates weave and dodge past their opponents and try to put a hard rubber disk called a puck into the other team's net. A goalie guards the net and tries to stop the puck.

Hockey players need good skating and passing skills. Players who disobey the rules of the game get a **penalty**. They must sit in the penalty box while their team plays **shorthanded**. Players wear a helmet on their head and protective padding on their legs, hips, shoulders, and elbows to prevent injuries when they crash into the boards, other players, or the ice.

*The player on the left is trying to **steal**, or take, the puck. Sometimes players **check**, or bump into, one another in order to steal it. Stealing and checking are part of the reason that hockey is an exciting game.*

J is for **jumping**. Jumping is part of many sports. Basketball players jump to dunk the ball in the basket. Runners jump over hurdles in races. Figure skaters jump to rotate in the air. Some sports are all about jumping. Long jump is a competition that involves jumping the greatest distance. High jump is a measure of who can jump the highest. Ski jumpers ski down a steep slope to gain speed and then take off into the air, jumping as far as 200 feet (60 m).

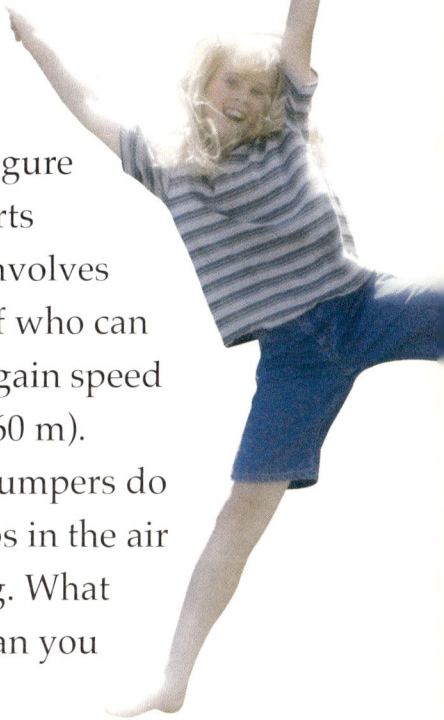

Freestyle ski jumpers do twists and flips in the air before landing. What other sports can you think of that include jumping?

This runner is jumping over a hurdle. He will leap over several hurdles in one race.

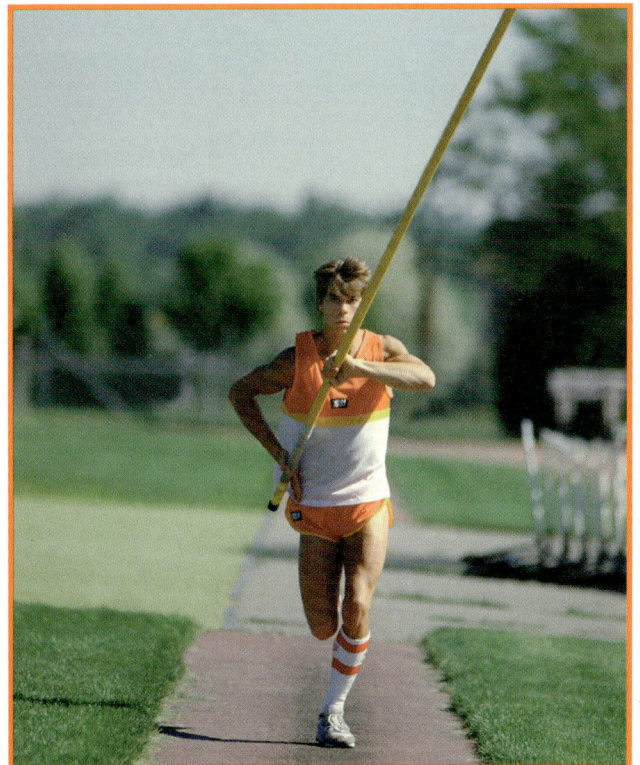

In the pole vault, jumpers use a long pole to help them sail over a high bar.

K is for **kayaking**. A kayak is a shallow, narrow boat that stays afloat in rough water. The first kayaks were made of sealskin and used by the Inuit. Today, kayaks are made of plastic or **fiberglass**. They are big enough for one or two riders to sit with their legs stretched out in front of them. The rider uses a paddle with a flat blade on each end to move and steer the kayak through the water. Kayaks are made to roll. They can flip upside down and turn over again.

*Kayak races are slalom events. The competitors have to pass around a number of poles called **gates** on their way down a fast-moving river. Kayak races take place in mountain rivers or in streams made by people. Competitors wear helmets and life vests for safety.*

is for **lacrosse**. Lacrosse was invented by Native North Americans. Players use wooden sticks with nets to catch, carry, and throw a small rubber ball. Teams score goals by putting the ball into the other team's net. Players can roll or hit the ball with their stick to score, but they are not allowed to kick it. In men's lacrosse, there are ten players from each team competing on the playing field, whereas women's games are played with twelve players.

*When Native North Americans played lacrosse, the **pitch**, or playing area, was many miles long. The game lasted several days and involved up to a thousand players! Today, lacrosse is played on a field that is sized similarly to a soccer field, and the game lasts about one hour.*

M is for **martial arts**. There are many types of martial arts such as karate, judo, aikido, and tae kwon do. People learn martial arts for many reasons. They want to learn self-defense, practice self-discipline, build their self-confidence, and compete in matches. Martial arts teach concentration, balance, and controlled movements.

(top) Even the youngest karate competitors participate in matches.
*(above) In karate matches, competitors **spar** with one another. Sparring means making fighting motions such as kicking and punching without actually hurting the other person.*

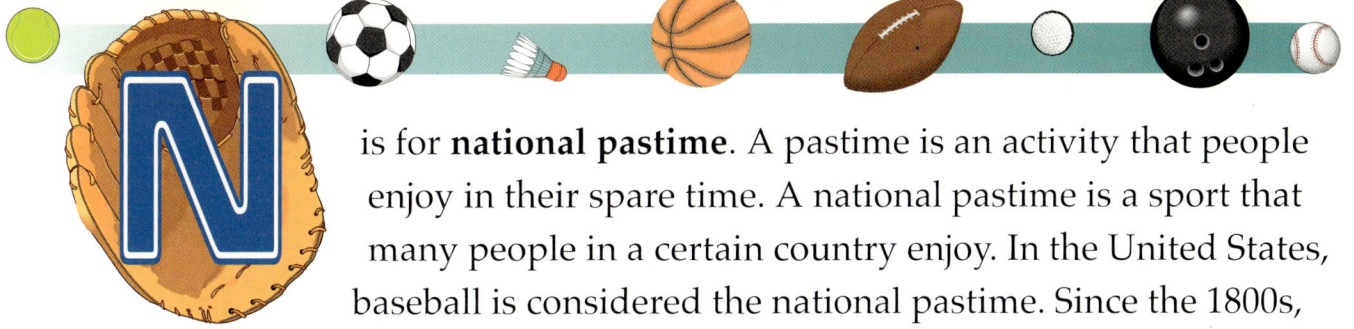

N is for **national pastime**. A pastime is an activity that people enjoy in their spare time. A national pastime is a sport that many people in a certain country enjoy. In the United States, baseball is considered the national pastime. Since the 1800s, North Americans have loved playing and watching baseball. In Canada, hockey is the number one sport, and in many European and South American countries, soccer is the most popular game.

*People of all ages love to play their favorite sport. Children play in leagues after school and in the summer. Groups of friends play in the park for fun. Some adults play **professionally**, or for money. People who love sports but do not play the game cheer on their favorite teams and players.*

O is for **Olympics**. The Olympic Games began in ancient Greece over 2000 years ago. The Greeks believed that physical fitness and competition honored the gods that they worshiped. Every four years they held competitions that included wrestling, running, and boxing.

The winter and summer Olympics are held every two years but with many more events. Athletes from around the world compete against one another for gold, silver, and bronze medals. Holding the Olympics is a way of bringing together the countries of the world. The goal of the Olympics is good **sportsmanship**. Many athletes dream of becoming Olympic-medal winners.

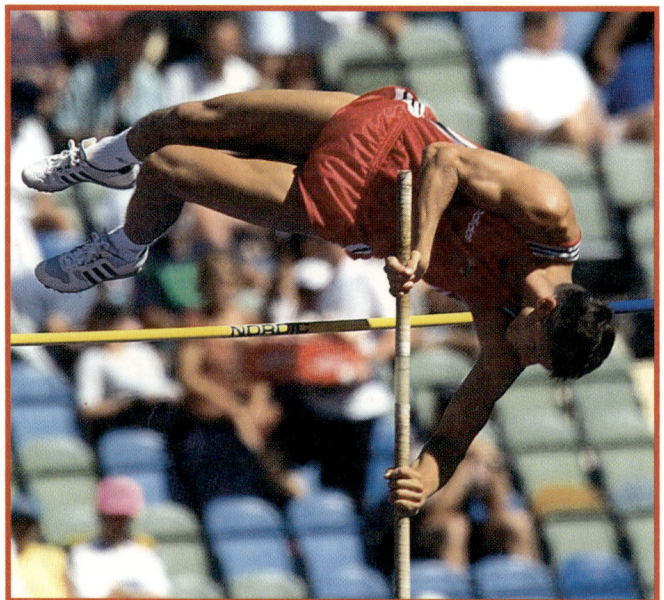

The summer Olympic Games include track and field (left and above), gymnastics, horse jumping, swimming, and tennis. Many Olympic events take place in a stadium. The track is used for races, and the infield is used for the field events. The opening and closing ceremonies also take place in the stadium.

(opposite page) A flame is lit during the opening of the summer and the winter games. It stays lit until the closing ceremonies.

The winter Olympics were first held in 1924 in France. Sports in the winter Olympics include ski jumping (above), figure skating (right), bobsledding (below), hockey, curling, and snowboarding.

P is for **Paralympics**. Paralympic Games are events in which athletes with physical disabilities compete. The Paralympics are held every two years. They take place at the site of the Olympics just after the Olympic Games are over. Paralympic athletes compete in the same types of events as Olympic athletes. They train for years to be in top physical condition in order to compete.

(left) Sledge hockey players sit on a sledge that has two blades for gliding over the ice.

(below) Wheelchairs for racing are built for speed. The large wheels help them move quickly.

is for **quiet**. Most people yell and cheer when they play or watch sports, but some sports require silence. Being quiet helps people think and concentrate. Golfers need silence in order to focus on hitting the ball. Gymnasts quietly concentrate on keeping their balance. Shhh! How quiet can you be? What games or activities do you play or do that require you to be quiet?

You have to be quiet while you are fishing so you do not scare away the fish. The only sound you hear when you fly a kite is the sound of wind ruffling the kite's tail.

R is for **rules**. To play a sport properly, you have to follow the rules of the game. Rules help keep sports safe and fair. In hockey, players are not allowed to raise their stick above their shoulders. In basketball, you cannot trip another player. These rules keep players from getting hurt. In baseball, the pitcher is not allowed to make cuts or marks on the ball in order to throw it faster or better. This action would not be fair to the opposing team.

(above) The tall hockey player is breaking the high-sticking rule. He will have to sit in the penalty box. (below) Referees make sure that players follow the rules and give out penalties if a rule is broken.

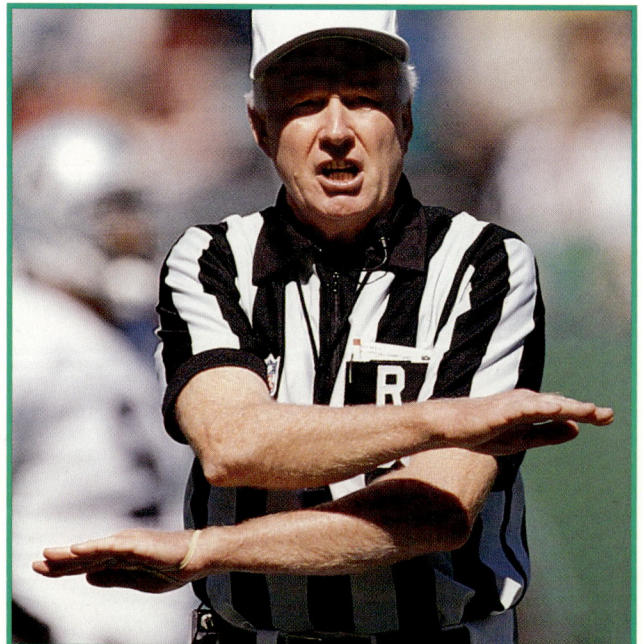

(above and right) Referees have uniforms that make them visible to the players and spectators. There are referees in every sport.

R is also for **rolling**. Rolling sports are speedy and exciting. Bicycling, inline skating, and skateboarding are all sports that get you rolling. Rolling on wheels takes balance and practice. Can you ride a two-wheeled bicycle? Maybe someday you will compete in a bike race or skateboarding competition.

Rolling is fast and fun, but it can also be dangerous. Inline skaters and skateboarders should always wear helmets and padding, especially when they perform their tricks.

S is for **soccer**. Soccer is the most popular sport in the world. It is played on a large field by two teams who try to kick a ball into each other's net. The players use their feet, knees, chest, and head to pass and shoot the ball. Soccer is called football in many countries because the players use their feet to kick the ball around the field. How is soccer different from the other sport called football?

(top left) Players try to keep the ball away from the other team. They want their team to have control of the ball.

(top right) This player is doing a high kick to pass the ball to a teammate.

(left) The goalie is the only player who tries to stop the ball with her hands. Gloves help protect her palms and improve her grip on the ball.

T is for **tennis**. Tennis players use a racket to hit a ball back and forth over a net. The net stretches across the middle of a court. Some people play **singles** tennis, which means one person plays against another person. In **doubles** tennis, a pair of people play against another pair. Points are scored when someone misses the ball or hits it out of bounds. "Love" is the term for a score of zero in tennis.

(right) "Out!" This player is letting her opponent know that the ball was hit out of the court bounds. She has just scored a point!

(bottom) The object of tennis is to hit the ball to an area of the court where your opponent will not be able to reach it. This player had to move quickly to hit the ball.

U is for **underwater sports**. Swimming is an underwater sport. Swimmers have to concentrate on their breathing and learn when to hold their breath as they race from one end of the pool to the other. At the end of each pool length, swimmers turn around underwater to save time. They blow out air as they turn so that water will not go up their nose. Synchronized swimmers spend long periods of time underwater. Scuba divers go deep underwater in oceans and lakes. They use an air tank to breathe and wear weights to keep them from floating to the surface.

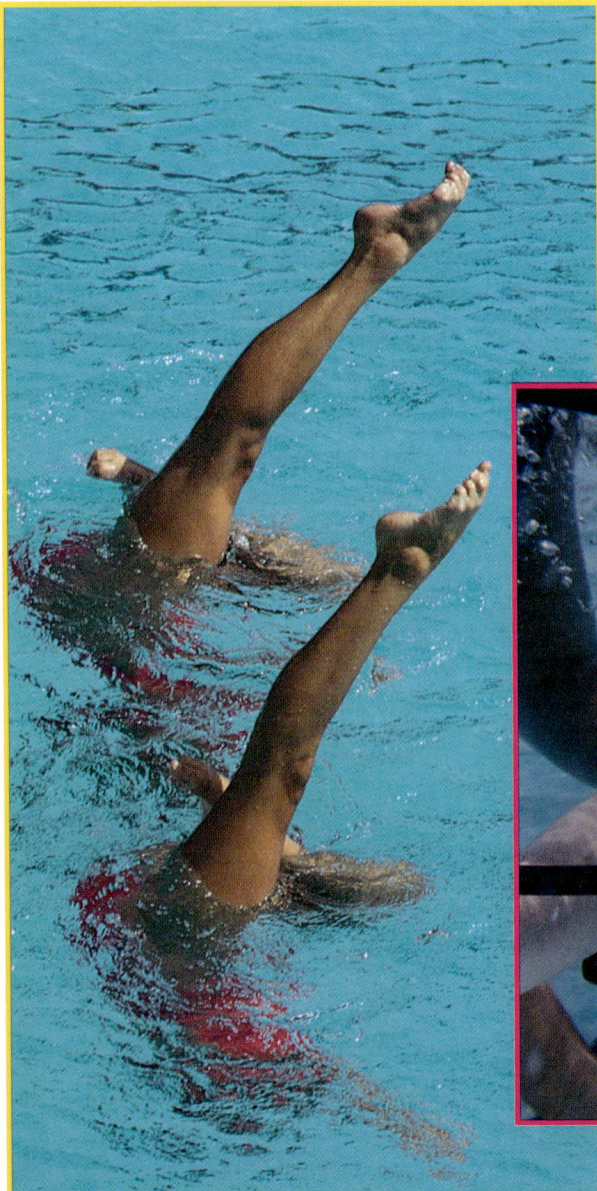

(left) These synchronized swimmers have to hold their breath while they hold difficult positions. They wear nose plugs to keep the water from going up their nose.

(below) This girl is learning how to scuba dive in a pool. She is practicing breathing with an air tank.

V is for **volleyball**. Volleyball is a team sport in which players hit a ball over a raised net with their hands. Each team tries to hit the ball to an area of the court from which their opponents will not be able to hit it back. Players wear elbow and knee pads because they often dive in order to hit the ball before it touches the floor or ground. Beach volleyball is played on outdoor sand courts. Have you ever played volleyball in a gymnasium or at the beach? How long can you **rally**, or keep the ball going back and forth without allowing it to bounce on the ground?

W

is for **wind sports**. In wind sports, people use the wind to give them power and speed. Windsurfing and sailing are wind sports that use large sails to catch the wind and push a windsurfer or sailboat across the surface of the water.

Windsurfers ride on large surfboards with a sail to race or perform stunts. They use their body weight to balance their sail against the strength of the wind. Some windsurfers compete in freestyle races in which they do spectacular jumps and flips over the water.

These windsurfers are competing in a race. The racers lean back and let the wind keep up their sail. They are following a course with markers. They must sail past the markers to reach the finish line.

X

is for **extreme sports**. Extreme sports are sports that are risky or dangerous. Bike races down steep mountains and skydiving from an airplane are examples of extreme sports. Most extreme-sport participants wear a helmet and padding for protection. Extreme sports are exciting but they cause many serious injuries!

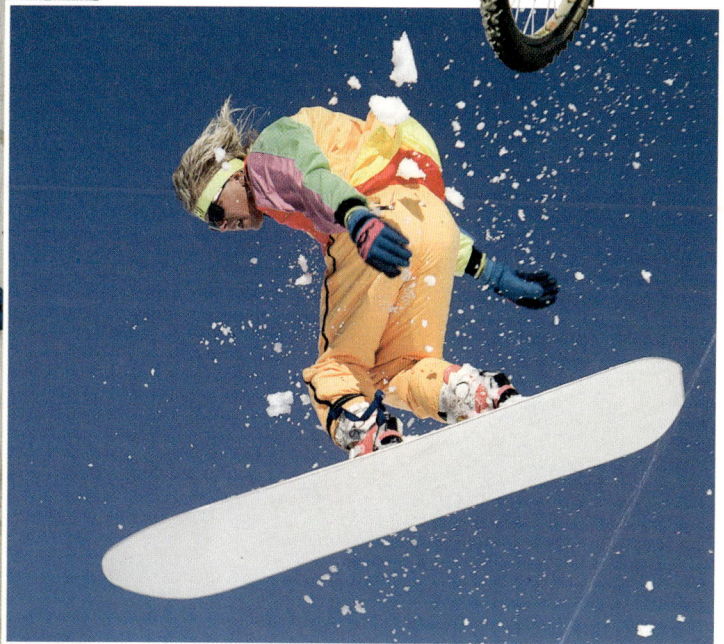

This girl is learning how to scale rocks on a climbing wall. She is wearing a harness to keep from falling.

Extreme-sports competitors perform daring tricks. Mountain bikers and snowboarders are judged on their turns and twists in the air.

Y is for **your favorite sport**.
What is your favorite sport? Is it one in which you have competed? How do you practice your sport? Which sports would you like to learn?

My favorite sport is skateboarding. I love to roll down the driveway on my stomach. My friends have their own favorite sports. Chiara loves mini-golf, Tammy practices football, and Max likes to fish with his dad.

Z is for **zero tolerance**. There is zero tolerance for breaking the rules in sports. One of the most important rules is that athletes cannot use drugs to help them perform better. At the Olympics, athletes are tested to make sure they have not been using drugs. When athletes are found to have used drugs, their medals are taken away from them.

These swimmers are Olympic gold-medal winners. Before they competed in their swimming event, they were tested to make sure they were not using drugs that would help them swim faster.

Words to know

apparatus A piece of equipment

athlete A person who trains for and participates in sports

contact sport A sport that involves forceful colliding or hitting

dressage Guiding a horse through several small and complex movements

equestrian A person who rides a horse; having to do with horseback riding

fiberglass A strong material that is made from millions of hardened threads of glass

freestyle Describing a sport that is performed with one's own style and level of difficulty

half-pipe A large curved ramp used for performing moves in some extreme sports

opponent A player from another team

penalty A punishment given to a player who has broken a rule

shorthanded Playing with fewer than the usual number of people

sportsmanship The behavior and attitude that a player displays while competing in a sporting event

stadium A large building with seats and a field in which sporting events are held

steeplechase A long horse race over an obstacle course

team sport A sport that involves a group of players competing against another group

tolerance The ability to put up with or allow something

trapeze A set of swings on long ropes on which acrobats perform tricks

Index

1 2 3 4 5 6 7 8 9 0   Printed in the U.S.A.   8 7 6 5 4 3 2 1 0 9